Prints

L G Clarke

India | USA | UK

Presentation by *BookLeaf Publishing*

Web: www.bookleafpub.com

E-mail: info@bookleafpub.com

ISBN: 9789360940843

First edition 2024

DEDICATION

To you

Tides

A small girl and her grandmother,
Silhouettes against low tide,
Hobbling, laughing,
Creating poems together,
Taking it in turns,
Each conjuring a line.

House Martins

I'm sat with you on the brow of a hill
in comfortable silence.
Coats beneath us.
The rain is clearing as we catch our breath,
watching house martins swoop and dip.
Their bellies white against a grey sky.

The Butterfly

3

We're sat having lunch.
We're raw as we grieve.
The tears flow unashamedly, free.
Over your shoulder,
The biggest butterfly I've ever seen.
Blue, iridescent, like a jewel, or the sea.
An escaped convict paying as little attention
to the rules as she.
You lean in, mischief in your eyes.
And just for a second, she's back.
An amazing, unexpected surprise.

Stars

Perfect, otherworldly, pinch me moments.
A slow kayak, deep ocean,
An inky pin pricked sky.
A mirror image of the water below -
Dark, never ending,
The swish of a paddle through phosphorescent;
warm hands on my shoulders,
As we bobbed in time.

Mud

5

It's dark.
And I feel the thick slickness of cool earth
beneath my feet,
Bare and keen,
As we gather in a hollow, like nomads,
like those who follow
some long forgotten druid order,
Our limbs stretching towards the sky as they
intertwine with ancient woodland elders,
Elated now they've found us.
The bass from the set echoes through my chest,
And I do my best to keep upright,
To make sense through the moonlight -
A woodland dance at midnight.

Queen Of The Forest

It seems so apt now,
that we should be two girls who met in the
woods.
and we really were girls -
both still teenagers.
Saplings.

We worked hard that summer.
It was hot.
and when it wasn't hot,
it was damp.
You over a steaming stove, me under a clammy
canopy.

So that afternoon,
when we took the kids,
to meet the ancient beech tree -
it was welcome relief.

She stood tall and proud -
rooted; confident.
Her fingertips spread assured towards the sky.
Her foundations ran deep below us, strong
enough to sit on.
Strong enough to carry others.

We craned our necks to take in her regality.
Her leaves emerald and dapped in the August
sun,
Her exterior cool and smooth,
Her stance poised and assertive.
With a following of sisters surrounding her,
equally resplendent but not quite as certain in
the world yet.

The Queen Of The Forest
So clearly, beautifully imbued
with an ancient wisdom
and timeless self assuredness.
She who danced when the storms blew hard
and refused to be knocked down.

It's been some time since then.
The Forest's Queen no doubt is stronger still.
I can't be sure.

What I am sure of,
As sure as she is sure of herself,
is that you are so much your own Queen my
friend.
I see so much of her in you.
You tackle life's storms with such a strong,
certain confidence.
You are so easily, naturally beautiful, so
grounded, so rooted.

So capable of supporting others;
Of sending secret underground support to your
sisters in need,
Souls who gravitate towards your peace.

So when the winds of life really howl
and perhaps winter isn't too far away,
I wish, more than anything,
for you to see yourself how others may.
Authentic, resplendent, wise,
Deserving of pride.

The Sea

You love me.
I know you love me.
But not in the same way you love her.

I don't hold your attention like she does...
curves and waves and natural, untamed beauty.
I definitely don't excite you like she does...
unpredictable; placid one day, joyful the next,
raging the day after.
But always, always beautiful.

I don't hold the same strength that you admire in
her.
She lures sailors, sinks ships, delights children,
inspires stories.

And I can't envy her.
I love her too, like some scared lunar sister,
drawn to her silent sorority.
She caresses, heals, soothes, supports.
She has held me countless times,
whether in adventure, or joy...
in fear, once or twice - when I underestimated
her -
Often just in peaceful stillness.

She has seen lovers arrive and disappear,
paddling across bioluminescent lakes,
reflecting stars, promising me the universe...
and she has seen my sisters rescue me,
scoop me up in solidarity, Sat in sunlight,
sand under our hands -
"How dare he do this, how dare he do that, you
deserve so much more..."
Platitudes? Compliments?
She has heard them,
seen them,
all.

You love her at her worst.
When she howls, thrashes, screams.
When she threatens to destroy everything you
have.
When she's bitter, salty, cold.
When she's flat, grey, uninspiring,
charmless.

You love her always.

She is as how all women, deep down,
I think, want to be.
Admired for who they truly are, but
respected, healthily.
Celebrated femininity.
Transparent but deep.

Capable of whispers but not allowing their
voice to be drowned.
Agency to speak.

Unapologetically themselves.
Night and day.
Making waves.

Soft Fruit

Our first kiss
was gentle.
Full and firm and sweet.
Like smoothing my lips
Against a plum
or a peach.

And with every delicious second, each
Exquisite minute,
I felt myself sinking deep,
descending,
falling,
like crisp Autumn leaves.

Not Their Usual Type

Do you know
How many men have told me
"I'm not their usual type"
Because my folds and rolls abundantly.
That they normally date smaller girls.
That they'll "make an exception" for me.

Do they know the sheer absurdity;
These men believed they could be less gentle
because there was more of me.
How hurtful it is to be attractive
solely because you're a novelty.

What's worse -
To be overlooked or fetishized?

I deserve to be loved at every size.

Lughnasadh

It's a Sunday afternoon in late summer.
The trains are running slower than usual,
and I chug, chug, chug along in a carriage that
idles through Wiltshire.

Crops are being harvested in a heatwave,
and I feel the satisfied warmth radiate
from golden patchwork,
as if I am wrapped in a towel having just swam
in the ocean,
now basking in a sunbeam.

Ashes

15

I thought I would love you forever,
But we evolved away from each other
into different people.
That's the thing they don't tell you about
heartbreak -
Sometimes you're wrenched away from the
flames
before you're ready.
And sometimes you are left
with smoldering ash,
having watched the fire burn out.

Sunlight

Lucy comes from the Latin word Lux,
which means light.
And this is something I have tried to embody -
A namesake I try to live by.

Not light as in a dove's feather,
or a snowflake,
or the paws of a cat,
or a whisper...

But light as in
boom bitches, here I am -
Glorious and radiant
and shining, unapologetically,
like the motherfucking sun.

Rope

You, my oldest friend, make me think of rope.
A belay, a safety line, a sacred thread
between now and our past.
You support and catch me.
Every time.

And sometimes, when I'm not ready to be saved,
and fight against you, the snap
and friction of your rescue stings -
But that doesn't mean I didn't need it.
It doesn't mean that you didn't know
what was best for me even when I didn't see
the fall coming.

Without the tension I know I have been
guilty of placing on you, you are soft and gentle,
flexible, relaxed.
I know, at times, I force you to be rough
and tense.
Safety nets have failed me in the past and
I am learning to put my complete faith in your
strength.
I know you've got me, but I am a heavy load.

Our threads are now so intertwined, so
co-woven,
That now I no longer know which stories
are yours and which are mine.
We have added to each other, over the years.
Because of you, the rope is as strong as I need it
to be.

I'll coil you up, neatly, and carry you with me
on every adventure.
You are essential.
You are tied to me and I to you.
Thank you for catching me when I fall.

John

It's the morning after.
You're sat, perched,
in your pants,
on a windowsill, up high.
Animated and excited,
you lean out of the window,
bare chested,
a cigarette in one hand,
the other,
brushing sleep from your eyes.

Fire

It's after sun down,
friends sit in the warm sand.
I reach out a hand to build the fire.
He says "there's enough -
next time, leave it to a man."

Vehement rage flickers within me,
An acrid response forming to rebuff his demand,
I want to embarrass him -
to hurt this neanderthal...

But I hold back,
people are looking.

I feel the red heat of angry surprise on my
cheeks.
that word.
enough.

You've eaten enough,
are you sure you're warm enough,
never being
enough.
I'm extinguished every time my embers try
to flicker into flames,

to burn,
to glow.

Simultaneously

Somebody always wants more from me -
more of me.
I'm smothered by expectations,
choked by opinions,
my throat scratched raw
holding back all the things I want to say.

Afterall,
it might dampen some man's ego...

No. Enough.

Hot white fury turns my stomach,
makes my palms sticky.
and my head spins
the blood pumping too loudly in my ears...

I get to my feet
and let him have it

Watermelons

22

How can you vilify children with stones?
You come with your military,
destroying their homes,
and they're the terrorists?

I'm asking God for guidance -
but I'm not sure that he exists.

Compass

I read a book once, about a girl, with a
golden compass.
She would ask it questions about the big things
in life,
And her golden compass would answer.

You, my dear friend, are my golden compass.
Forever accepting, listening, guiding me,
through my
"What ifs?"
My "Whys?', my "Hows?"
My "I don't fucking get its."
No question is ever too much, too strange,
too out there.
No time is ever inconvenient,
inappropriate or wrong.
You make time.
Perhaps you are also a pocket watch?
Sacred, spiritual, analogue cogs,
Forever tick tick ticking over the important
things.

You have this talent
deep in your bones.

You provide lost souls with direction.

24

Mothers

Our mothers -
They wear shame like a well loved jacket.
But this world of self-hatred, we have to unpack
it.

You are made up of light and abundance
and cosmic energy,
You are not some predetermined body
a fuck boy said you should be.
And all these beauty standards,
We can reject them,
Take up space,
and compliments,
learn to expect them.
You are radiant and stellar and bright,
and those too dim to stand in your light -
Honey, it's their problem.
You're too busy shining, you already forgot
them.
Take up space, demand to be heard
and know your worth.
For your divine purpose here upon this earth,
Whatever it may turn out to be,
Is not to look beautiful.

It is to be free.

Imposter Syndrome

I think I'm a fraud,
Masquerading and anxious,
A pretend adult.

What Is Talent?

Is it something tactile, bottled and sold?
Or something auspicious, secret and old?
Is it luck, just luck, and not much else?
Is it effort? Are we to rely on ourselves?
It is nothing that can be explained or defined?
Or is it simply a matter of time?